TRUMPED OUT

Asher Andrews

ISBN 978-0-359-03815-2

PRINTED IN THE UNITED STATES OF AMERICA

Editing and Design by Asher Andrews

Published by Asher Andrews

asherandrews@outlook.com

To my son Asher, for whom I have the highest hopes.

CONTENTS

9 Acknowledgements

11 Introduction

15 Are We A Christian Nation?

19 Gender, Race & Sexual Orientation

23 Immigration

27 Abortion

31 Education

33 American Culture

37 English

41 Unemployment

45 Social Security

49 Liberal Persecution Complex

55 Black Lives Matter

63 Family

65 Love

67 Truth

ACKNOWLEDGEMENTS

I am writing this book under the auspices of preserving human dignity, charity, kindness, wisdom, truth and liberty. I am so very thankful to my family for a lifetime of support. To our Father in Heaven, I thank you for giving me the encouragement and tools to write this book and to be of some use for Your purpose.

INTRODUCTION

Corinthians 2:12-18

Having therefore such a hope, we use great boldness in our speech, and are not as Moses, who used to put a veil over his face that the sons of Israel might not look intently at the end of what was fading away. But their minds were hardened; for until this very day at the reading of the old covenant the same veil remains unlifted, because it is removed in Christ. But to this day whenever Moses is read, a veil lies over their heart; but whenever a man turns to the Lord, the veil is taken away. Now the Lord is the Spirit; and where the Spirit of the Lord is, there is liberty. But we all, with unveiled face beholding as in a mirror the glory of the Lord, are being transformed into the same image from glory to glory, just as from the Lord, the Spirit.

-New American Standard Bible

ARE WE A CHRISTIAN NATION?

Yes we are.

We have always been and still are a Christian nation and we owe our liberty and the preservation of what liberties remain, to that fact. According to a 2014 study by the Pew Research Center, 70.6% of Americans identify as Christian. Not only are we a Christian nation now but our country was founded under God's authority which is cited in the Declaration of Independence. Without God's authority, there is no sovereign and independent "United States of America".

The introduction of the Declaration of Independence states, "When in the Course of human events, it becomes necessary for one people to dissolve the political bands which have connected them with another, and to assume among the powers of the earth, *the separate and equal station to which the Laws of Nature and of Nature's God entitle them*, a decent respect to the opinions of mankind requires that they should declare the causes which impel them to the separation."

<u>The preamble states</u>, "We hold these truths to be self-evident, that all men are created equal, that they are *endowed by their Creator with certain unalienable Rights*, that among these are Life, Liberty and the pursuit of Happiness."

<u>The conclusion states</u>, "We, therefore, the Representatives of the united States of America, in General Congress, Assembled, *appealing to the Supreme Judge of the world for the rectitude of our intentions*, do, in the Name, and by Authority of the good People of these Colonies, solemnly publish and declare, That these united Colonies are, and of Right ought to be Free and Independent States; that they are Absolved from all Allegiance to the British Crown, and that all political connection between them and the State of Great Britain, is and ought to be totally dissolved; and that as Free and Independent States, they have full Power to levy War, conclude Peace, contract Alliances, establish Commerce, and to do all other Acts and Things which Independent States may of right do. And for

the support of this Declaration, *with a firm reliance on the protection of divine Providence*, we mutually pledge to each other our Lives, our Fortunes and our sacred Honor."

These are 4 very clear references to the Christian God of the authors of the Declaration of Independence. 1. *"the Laws of Nature and of Nature's God"* 2. *"their Creator"* 3. *"the Supreme Judge of the world"* 4. *"the protection of divine Providence"*

It must be clearly stated that the Declaration of Independence is not just establishing a free and independent state but, is also a covenant or agreement between that independent state and the Christian God of that document's writers, their Creator, Nature's God, The Supreme Judge of the World. For by acknowledging their Christian God as the source of our human right (among others) to have established the United States of America under protection of Divine Providence, we thusly must accept that our existence and continued protection are dependent on our faith in God. If we say that God does not exist, then the authority for creating the United States of America also never existed and we are still under the rule of the crown. If we say that God does not exist then we also will lose the protection of God's "Divine Providence" which has kept us safe from our enemies for so long. That protection will wholly and completely disappear if we do not return to our Christian principles of; faith in God, respect for human dignity, charity and kindness, wisdom, truth and liberty. We have had only brief demonstrations of this protection being lifted, in God's mercy he has spared us from complete destruction that we might return to Him, but the time is not long before that protection vanishes if we do not open our hearts to the truth.

GENDER, RACE & SEXUAL ORIENTATION

Should a human being be given special privileges, grants, allowances or consideration because of their gender, race, sexual orientation or other classification of human? Absolutely not.

Galatians 3:26-29

"For ye are all sons of God through faith in Christ Jesus. For all of you who were baptized into Christ have clothed yourselves with Christ. There is neither Jew nor Greek, there is neither slave nor free man, there is neither male nor female; for you are all one in Christ Jesus. And if you belong to Christ, then you are Abraham's offspring, heirs according to promise.

-New American Standard Bible

It is the epitome of injustice to give preference to a man simply because he is a man or preference to a person of English heritage simply because their ancestors were from England, and so on and so forth with each variety of human being that a government, human or institution can fabricate. If a human is oppressed then the answer to that oppression is to stop doing it or intervene so that the oppression might be stopped, that's it. It is enough to simply stop the oppression, attempts to somehow compensate for an oppression simply results in more oppression. The question of race/ethnicity, gender, sexual orientation or other classification of human ought never be considered in reference to employment, education, grants, tax status or any other public endeavor or activity. We live in a society teeming with discriminatory practices and rife with a lack of understanding about the injustice committed when we; promote a less qualified person over another in the workplace simply for being a certain gender, admit a less qualified candidate into a university for declaring themselves to be of a particular ethnic heritage, tolerate discriminatory words being uttered from a person of a particular ethnicity or sexual orientation simply because of their subclass of human. It is the mission of injustice to create classifications of human, which imply that the person is subhuman and somehow not worthy of the liberty God so generously has given us. It's easier to marginalize and control and ultimately oppress humans if they are not of a united front. By creating subhuman classifications, injustice creates an us versus them mentality among categories of human and can oppress everyone gradually by simply oppressing a subhuman category one at a time. The eventual result being that everyone suffers oppression. That the liberty and sovereignty of the individual is eroded and eliminated and we are playing right into it, every day. We must abandon this sort of group classification syndrome, it's good enough to just be American.

In 1959 @ 87 years old, Bertrand Russel was asked a question by John Freeman for BBC's Face to Face. That question was, "What would you think it's worth telling future generations about the life you've lived and the lessons you've learned from it?" Bertrand Russel's response was, "I should like to say two things, one intellectual and one moral. The intellectual thing I should want to say to them is this: when you are studying any matter, or considering any philosophy, ask yourself only 'what are the facts?' and 'what is the truth that the facts bear out?' Never let yourself be diverted either by what you wish to believe or by what you think would have beneficent social effects if it were believed, but look only and solely at, what are the facts. That is the intellectual thing that I should wish to say. The moral thing I wish to say to them is very simple. Love is wise, hatred is foolish. In this world which is getting more and more closely interconnected, we have to learn to tolerate each other. We have to learn to put up with the fact that some people say things that we don't like. We can only live together in that way and if we are to live together and not die together, we must learn a kind of charity and a kind of tolerance, which is absolutely vital to the continuation of human life on this planet."

IMMIGRATION

Ban all immigration immediately.

 Without exception we must cease all immigration immediately. Illegal entry into the United States of America ought never be tolerated and extreme force must be used to defend against illegal entry. We cannot be strong let alone function and endure the challenges of time if we willfully allow our core American beliefs to be undermined. We have been given a great gift by our creator and the human creators of this country, and a great responsibility to care for that gift. We have been reckless with that gift. We were busy with the advent of modern convenience, cultivated a lust for war and were willfully blinded by consumerism and tactful marketing strategies. We were misled by charismatic leaders all the while riding on the coat tails of those who fought and died to pass this gift along to us. We silently, gradually and persistently have had nearly every act of human endeavor restricted and controlled under the guise of safety or security while the most important factors in our safety and security (our borders and culture) were not just ignored but actively destroyed. America's border policy is its greatest act of self-harm in the last century, greater even than our penchant for aggressive occupation of foreign nations. Enforcement of our borders must be extreme and immediate. We must provide a path to citizenship for those who are here right now as I write this book, not in a month or a year from now, but as of February 2017. The path to citizenship must only be offered to those of good conduct, not perfect conduct but good conduct and not past conduct but of present conduct. After our borders are protected under threat of force, we must empty our prisons and jails of people who are here illegally and serving a sentence greater than one year and return them to their country of origin. Not when their sentence is complete but immediately after our borders are secure. The first and most basic act of self-defense against foreign harm is observing our own borders. For a nation with so many citizens who are lazy in their faith or who vehemently hate religion, it is an astounding demonstration of God's mercy that we still even have a border to protect. In spite of ourselves and the rampant iniquity we commit on one another, God has still maintained the covenant made with our founders via the Declaration of Independence. We still have a chance to turn things around if we repent, return to our faith and begin caring for our gift and humanitie's gift which is, the United States of America. If the United States as we know it falls, the entire world will suffer.

Acts 17:26

From one man, He created all the nations throughout the whole earth. He decided beforehand when they should rise and fall, and He determined their boundaries.

-The New Living Translation Bible

ABORTION

Should it be illegal and is it wrong? It is illegal and of course it is wrong.

Our rights ought never be infringed upon. Our right to do what we want with our bodies is God given and any law infringing upon that right is unjust and ironically unlawful. The only caveat to that is if our expression of that right infringes on another human's right or involves their property. A human's life right supersedes another human's property right. Since a human has a right to their own life you cannot legally take that without their consent and they will not be able to give that consent until 18 years after their birth, depending on the state. Even if a human gives you consent to take their life, it would be considered murder in most circumstances. An abortion is also an act of violence on a human's body, and a body is that human's property, abortion violates a human being's property and life rights. Killing unwanted humans probably makes situations easier to handle, probably reduces crime, certainly makes a prospective parent's life easier and saves tax payers and humans a significant amount of money. It doesn't change the fact that a human has a right to their property and their life. It's a lot easier to dismiss that truth than deal with an unwanted human. Another factor to consider is sometimes rights conflict. When a developing human being alters their mother's body and it's functions, they are affecting the mother's property and probably even damaging it, however, they are not usually infringing on the mother's right to live. When one life jeopardizes the life of another then we must do everything we can do to rescue both lives. One life does not have a greater right to exist than another. Even if one is an aggressor, we have a moral responsibility to try to avoid killing the aggressor by running away, fighting or finding shelter and so on. The above answers the legal question of abortion and whether it's lawful or unlawful. Now I will answer the moral question, is it wrong? Perhaps the most significant implication of abortion is not that one life is killed or even that tens of millions of lives are killed in the United States of America via abortion. It is that abortion destroys human dignity. Humanity will not survive the complications of its own existence without respect for human dignity and divine intervention. In the acknowledgements, I defined the auspices under which I write this book. I write under the auspices of preserving human dignity, charity, kindness, wisdom, truth and liberty. There is nothing kind or charitable about abortion. There is nothing wise about allowing abortion to occur as it devalues our very existence. There is a blatant lie being propagated about abortion which is that a human being inside of its mother is not a human being. It is incalculable how many lives are destroyed out of ignorance of the truth, and how many women were preyed upon and deceived by a movement they did not truly understand. There are still women out there who are not aware that much of their oral contraceptive works by inducing an abortion. We have been lied to or lie to ourselves in an incalculable number of abortions in order to mitigate the consequences of our own promiscuity. On average $500,000,000.00 per year is taken from you and given to the nation's largest entity which commits abortions.

EDUCATION

Education is a function of the individual state to the capacity of its choosing and the federal government ought to have no involvement.

 States alone have the burden and freedom to govern the educational standards and practices of its citizens. Each state is unique and has a unique workforce, ambitions, resources and citizenry. The individual state is most fit to assess its own educational aspirations and needs. Rather than having to satisfy the vastly diverse range of challenges and aspirations of 49 other states, the individual state can efficiently hone its educational doctrine to best suit its own population. Californians have different educational challenges and aspiration than Iowans. How can we pretend a state can be competently served best to maximize their individual success under one doctrine which is so general as to include 49 other states? In 2015, the United States spent $80,900,000,000.00 on education. Money which never should have been taken from the states to begin with and then they distributed that money unequally amongst the United States and it's territories. Ultimately, a child's education is the responsibility of their parents. It's not yours or mine unless we are volunteering our time or money to assist a parent in doing so.

AMERICAN CULTURE

Our culture must be preserved. It is what established this country and it is what has made the United States of America a success while the countries of other cultures have failed.

We have been enormously successful to an unprecedented degree and it is because of our culture. We have seen the rise and fall of powerful empires like Russia and Germany and we were left standing. Libya, Egypt, Iraq, Afghanistan and Ethiopia, among others, do not have our stability and resolve in part because of our activities in and around them, but also because of their culture. A country is its culture, and the people are what define a culture. It's very simple, if you alter the demographic of a nation with foreign beliefs and attitudes then you are undermining its culture and changing that country, albeit quietly. Consistency in culture should once again be promoted. The pledge of allegiance is/was a unifying ritual which acknowledged who we are as the American culture. The promotion of many subcultures to which a person can choose to identify so we can be further classified and separated is a fantastic example of divide and conquer. These people go here, these people go there, and one doesn't like what the other says and now everyone is arguing about everything except how to fix the actual problems. Problems concerning race are not actual problems. They are invented problems and people love picking sides. The same is true for gender disparities and any other groups engaging in social warfare. It is a hurtful subversion of human dignity to pretend we are all the same in our challenges, and people often ignore or deny the self-inflicted damage caused when a person chooses to identify with subcultural beliefs. They not only cause themselves harm but then demand the rest of us not just find that decision acceptable, but we must also enable them to engage in the activities of that subculture. If we object we are labeled a bigot. At some point in our lives we all choose who or what we will serve, what we value and how we speak to others and about others. Often times people blame the subculture which they choose to identify with as the cause of their troubles and conveniently think this removes them from the responsibility of their predicament. It does not. My point with this is that we ought to promote a consistent culture, core values, core beliefs and allow individual expression of their faith at home, in the workplace and in public as a part of promoting our culture. Liberty is a key value in our culture, which has been greatly eroded in the last 20 years. It has nothing to do with not having a diverse enough culture and everything to do with our culture being undermined actively and passively. There is only one American culture and that is you and me and our families acting in harmony with our founder's intentions to defend our individual rights and liberties. We care for one another and treat one another with dignity and have the courage to discard untruths.

ENGLISH

English is our language and part of our cultural identity. It is the responsibility of every physically and neurologically capable person to know.

According to Census bureau data from 2013, the American Community Survey tells us that there are 61,800,000 US citizens who speak another language at home and only 25,100,000 of these speak English very well. On May 18th 2006 at 5pm the 109th Congress Agreed to S.Amdt. 4064 to S.2611 titled Comprehensive Immigration Reform Act of 2006 (CIRA). The purpose of the amendment to CIRA was to declare English as the national language of the United States of America and to promote the patriotic integration of prospective citizens. It's a fantastic move by our leaders, and if everyone spoke English this would promote human dignity, unity, kindness, and along with spreading wisdom and truth it would liberate those who formerly did not speak English. If everyone here spoke English tomorrow, it would be the single most unifying event in America since September 11th 2001. Yet not everyone in America speaks English. Why? Certainly not for lack of assistance and ability to learn. It's thanks in part to enabling behaviors of businesses and institutions, apathy on the part of the individual and lack of understanding of how much potential could be unlocked by non-English speakers simply being able to effectively communicate with the majority of their fellow citizens. Ignorance of our language is inherently divisive. It not only prevents unity, but actively divides us. It causes anger and frustration, prevents relationships from developing and causes confusion and misunderstanding. The lack of the ability to communicate oppresses the individual and prevents them from realizing the very best our country has to offer. There is a group of oppressors who seek to enable the non-English speaking person to continue in their ignorance and undermine their potential and our social structure via the false pretense of assisting the ignorant by providing multilingual material and signs or even interpreters. To promote unity, human dignity, truth and liberty among our citizens, we must all be able to effectively communicate in English. We should not tolerate oppressive behaviors such as enabling. Enabling always creates dependence and dependence is not liberty.

UNEMPLOYMENT

Everyone who wants to work can work. Eliminate immigration and the problem of unemployment will be eliminated.

Without the massive immigration numbers we've experienced over the last 30 years there's another thing we could have gone without experiencing, unemployment and meager wages. In 2015 the American Community Survey calculates that there were a total of 42,400,000 legal and illegal immigrants residing in the United States. That doesn't even factor in the children they had who have now entered the workforce. According to the Pew Research Center there were 11,400,000 people unlawfully residing in the United States. Who can blame anyone for wanting to come to the greatest country in the world? Employers have gotten away for so long and with so little consequence for hiring people who are breaking the law by being here. This reminds me of the signs in parks which say, "DON'T FEED THE GEESE". Which is akin to saying, "DON'T ENABLE

THE GEESE". According to the Ohio State University College of Food, Agricultural and Environmental Sciences, when people feed Canada geese, it is a major cause of human–Canada goose conflict, they go on to say, "Cessation of any feeding that may be occurring is crucial to reducing conflicts and damage. Creation and enforcement of no-feeding ordinances are highly recommended." I would like to add that feeding geese also prevents their migration and causes them to displace the local wildlife population. This phenomenon occurs in human populations as well. When we enable humans who should not be here to continue being here, they tend not to want to leave and they displace American citizens in the work force through overpopulating the supply of laborers and other workers. They also eviscerate any presumed competition amongst businesses to provide a competitive and reasonable wage. Their presence in the workforce increases the supply without increasing demand which makes the average American worker less valuable. This discourages some Americans from entering or reentering the workforce and contributes to unemployment. This effect of immigration into the United States of America is obvious and is the number one factor in unemployment.

SOCIAL SECURITY

People who are mentally and physically capable of speaking English should speak English to receive benefits and contributing to the system should be optional for the private citizen.

We have worked very hard for what we have, in my case alone my employers (on my behalf) and I have paid $73,126.00 into Social Security and Medicare, I'm 36 by the way. Let's pretend for a moment that the individual were responsible to provide for their own retirement. If I were to take that $73,126.00 and could invest it into an IRA with a 7 percent return I would have $264,462.00 at age 55 if I never again contributed to it. It's not a fantastic amount of money but it is a phenomenally better return than putting it into the mismanaged system which currently exists. It is absolutely outrageous that we are forced to contribute to a system which may or may not ever be there should we become disabled or upon retirement age. In 2016 the president's proposed budget for Social

Security, Unemployment & Labor, Medicare & Health accounted for $2,475,100,000,000.00. That's over half the budget plan for 2016 in the United States of America and if spread evenly over every man woman and child in the US would burden us each with over $7000 just for 2016, half of which would be paid for by employers. I'm not making a judgement on whether or not the individual beneficiaries of these benefits are abusing them, nor am I saying they do or do not deserve them, what I am saying is that we should not be forced to contribute to a Ponzi scheme and that we can better manage and customize our financial planning individually. Yes this involves personal financial responsibility and if someone wants to participate in the aforementioned Ponzi scheme then they should be allowed to. As for the part about speaking English. According to a letter published by the Washington Free Beacon from Senator Jeff Sessions to the Acting Commissioner of the Social Security Administration Carolyn Colvin, individuals who cannot speak English are fast tracked for approval. According to the Washington Free Beacon article describing the letter:

"Sessions said, 'there are only two questions asked at hearings, including, 'Can you speak and understand English?' and 'Can you read and understand English?'

If the applicant answers 'no' to these questions, the [Administrative Law Judge] does not probe any further,' he said." That is absolutely disgusting. I do not have information providing statistics on the actual number of Social Security claims which are approved on that basis but if it is 1 then it is a misappropriation, it is simply theft from an already unsustainable system. The solution to that injustice is simple, applicants for Social Security Disability must speak English if they are mentally and physically able to learn English. Not speaking English in America is a major barrier to employment. In all likelihood if the person applying for Social Security Disability were able to speak English then they might actually be able to work.

LIBERAL PERSECUTION COMPLEX

Liberals have an interest in fabricating the appearance of being persecuted for the purpose of creating laws which support their beliefs and taking money from all of us to spend on their special interests.

Without persecution the liberal agenda is just a group of people wanting laws and money for causes which increase scope of government and limit personal and religious freedoms. Furthermore, absent having the appearance of being persecuted or that their fellow Americans are being persecuted, Americans would not tolerate their freedoms and culture being undermined. It is so very tempting for each one of us to succumb to the notion that the challenges and consequences in life are due to the actions of someone else. It's a lot easier for us to blame another person or institution for our challenges than it is to change our behavior or to stop being part of a self-destructive cultural ideology. A key mechanism of the liberal agenda is Racism. Liberals have convinced many ethnic minorities in the United States of America that their problems are not due to cultural beliefs and individual behavior but that the white establishment and white people are/is conspiring against them. The fact is that the liberal establishment and white liberals (and liberals of every gender and ethnicity) ARE conspiring against minorities and creating very tempting pathways for minorities to become dependent upon a liberal government institution. Minorities who do not need or want assistance are easily persuaded into believing that their family members and they too would have so much more if only the white problem could be mitigated in some way. This is done under the guise of help and relief from their white male oppressors. Another liberal campaign is to seduce women into believing that they are oppressed in two major ways. That men are causing women to make less money than men for doing the same amount of work and that the male dominated political landscape is telling women what they can or cannot do with their bodies. These arguments are another lie. I don't know of any job where the pay scale is based on gender. It's simply a fictitious argument.

There are a number of factors as to why men on average are paid more than women but it has nothing to do with oppressing women. The most obvious factor is that women are the mothers of the world and on average spend more time away from work. People often elect not to take promotions which would demand a greater devotion of time spent at work especially in the case of single parents who are primary caretakers of their children. According to a 2011 article published in the Huffington Post by Robert Hughes, Jr. approximately 68-88 percent of primary caretakers of children are women. The other way liberals take advantage of women via sexism is by telling women that committing an abortion is their right and that men are suppressing women's right to do as they wish with their own body by restricting or banning abortion. Banning abortion is not about restricting a woman's right to do anything. Banning abortion is about protecting the human rights of the baby inside her. Sometimes two humans arrive at conflict when one chooses to express their rights. In the case of abortion, the right of the mother to do as she pleases with her person conflicts with the right of the unborn human being to their life. The right to life supersedes any property right and supersedes the right for a person to do as they choose with their body. Liberals are anti-American. Liberals pander to every American by giving them something to hate in unison, themselves, themselves vicariously through their hate for America. Liberals attempt to entice American citizens into believing their problems are a result of persecution from the white, male, Judeo-Christian establishment. What if you don't have problems? That's okay they include problemless citizens too, by guilting them into realizing that the America they so love has oppressed untold millions of disadvantaged American citizens. White guilt and white privilege have paid major dividends in enabling liberals to undermine American values, culture and law. Finally This leads us into the liberal antiChristian and anti-Semitic agenda. Separating people into different categories, allowing them to kill unborn children and convincing them that America is their oppressor is inconsistent with the core tenets of Judaism and Christianity. If people believe in a

Judeo-Christian God, they cannot also believe in an ideology which undermines their faith unless they are a liar or overt hypocrite. The attack on Judeo-Christian beliefs must be successful for the liberal agenda to work because none of the other tactics will work on honest people if they do not abandon Judeo-Christian theology. It is worthy to note that according to the first amendment of the Constitution of the United States of America, "Congress shall make no law respecting an establishment of religion, or prohibiting the exercise thereof..." Liberal tactics are racist, sexist, antiChristian, anti-Semitic and anti-American. These are four very terrible and dangerous aspects of liberal tactics and people know they are outright evil. How is it possible at this day and age that people would want to identify with these abhorrent traits? It's simple, the tactics are disguised as something else.

BLACK LIVES MATTER

Black Lives Matter is a racist, anti-law enforcement, anti-African American, terrorist organization.

There is nothing more divisive in American culture than the intentional propagation and perpetuation of black vs white racism. Racism is so effective and easy to use as a tool to gain interest in a cause. The minor challenge is to figure out how to apply it to a cause. The cause of Black Lives Matter according to it's website reads as follows, "Black Lives Matter is an ideological and political intervention in a world where Black lives are systematically and intentionally targeted for demise. It is an affirmation of Black folks' contributions to this society, our humanity, and our resilience in the face of deadly oppression." The stated goal of Black Lives Matter is ambiguous, but the key liberal tactic is obvious, citing oppression. While the website failed to provide an exact problem and solution it was wildly successful in recruiting privileged white guilt and black racism into hate toward law enforcement, government, and white people. How was this accomplished? By exploiting the appalling circumstances in the death of Trayvon Martin. I believe the creators of Black Lives Matter were racist well before they chose to exploit the tragic homicide of Trayvon Martin. Trayvon Martin was killed by George Zimmerman, a man of Peruvian, African and German descent. George Zimmerman is described as Hispanic on his voter registration. The media famously sensationalized the homicide as a white on black killing and is responsible for intentionally disseminating disinformation to the public to generate strong feelings which then generated viewership. The ethnicity of the two people involved does not change the circumstances nor the fact that a young man is now dead because of them. Americans who think they are pointing out the hypocrisy of Black Lives Matter by citing statistics of black on black crime are not understanding the point of Black Lives Matter. The name "Black Lives Matter" is a distraction and disguise to what Black Lives Matter is. Saving and improving the quality of life of Americans of African descent is not what Black Lives Matter is all about, it's about providing a venue for racism and exploiting a young black man's homicide to legitimize black on white racism and hatred toward law enforcement. Black Lives Matter is correct in their position that black on black crime has nothing to do with their grievances or anything to do with their purpose. Saving black lives has nothing to do with their purpose. The group proves this by ignoring the overwhelmingly largest group of murderers of black citizens which is black men. Again, their purpose is to provide a venue for black on white racism and hatred toward law enforcement. Black Lives Matter is undermining and ignoring the power of the African American community to solve its problems and is the single greatest enemy to Americans of African descent. Black Lives Matter is a harmful distraction and does an incredible and effective disservice to solving the problems of the black community. It dissuades the sympathy and interest of many Americans who might otherwise contribute to solving the problems and concerns of the black community. This is why and how Black Lives Matter is an anti-African American organization. Black Lives Matters is anti-law enforcement. In an interview with Ari Shapiro (NPR), Patrisse Cullors of Black Lives Matter stated her desired result of Black Lives Matter which is, "Defunding police departments". My opinion is that she wants law enforcement agencies defunded because she hates law enforcement. She wants defunding to lay off officers and minimize the number of police contacts with black citizens in spite of the fact that it would have a horrendous effect on the communities who most need the protection of law enforcement. Defunding law enforcement would increase victimization of the black community and cause more black lives to be lost at the hands of criminals who know they would have a much lower chance of being caught. The idea of defunding police departments is ironic since Black Lives Matter protests have a history of becoming violent and in need of law enforcement presence and intervnetion as in San Diego, St.Paul, Charlotte, Milwaukee, Indiana University, Washington D.C. and others. If you want defunding of police agencies then why on earth would you support activities which increase demand for them. This exacerbates law enforcement resources and gives agencies very valid reasons for requesting increasing funds. Thanks in part to Black Lives Matter and the violence they incite these agencies will get it. Black Lives Matter also has inspired the targeting of officers which further increases demand for funding of new protective equipment and more officers which will ultimately result in more police contact with citizens. Again, I believe Patrisse Cullors and Black Lives Matter is lying and they want to promote black on white racism and that is it. That's why the behavior of Black Lives Matter supporters will never be consistent with the organization's expressed intent. It's simply because representatives of Black Lives Matter cannot openly express the organizations true purpose which I believe is to provide a venue for black on white racism and anti law enforcement sympathies. Milwaukee County Sheriff David Clarke views Black Lives Matter as a hate group, which is correct but I believe it may also be a terrorist subnational group according to Title 22 of the U.S. Code, Section 2656f(d) which defines terrorism as, "premeditated, politically motivated violence perpetrated against noncombatant targets by subnational groups or clandestine agents, usually intended to influence an audience." My biggest concern about the ultimate impact of Black Lives Matter is that they are inciting racism among all ethnicities. The public misinterprets the agenda of Black Lives Matter as being the agenda of all black Americans. This confusion is making a lot of people angry with the black community. Black Lives Matter is systematically alienating the black community from the otherwise willing assistance of many Americans and our government. Black Lives Matter has alienated, angered and offended; women, law enforcement officers, white Americans and homosexuals by referring to them as "queer" multiple times on the Black Lives Matter website. In the Black Lives Matter manifesto they also alienated Jews by accusing Israel of "genocide" and "apartheid". Perhaps most ironically, they alienated many African Americans as well by forcing them to be vicariously associated with a black racist subnational group which they want nothing to do with. Black Lives Matter is not synonymous with "black American", nor will it ever be.

FAMILY

Intact families are the most important factor relating to a child's success in life and is the primary corollary in the prevention of crime among American citizens.

I consider an intact family to be a mother and father free of substance abuse issues who coexist in a household free of abuse toward one another with all of their children in their custody until those children are at least 18 years of age. We all have met American citizens in our lives, usually hundreds if not thousands of them and there is an obvious and common theme which emerges. People who engage in or who have engaged in criminal activity have commonly experienced a childhood lacking the structure and security of an intact family. Conversely, people who do not engage in criminal activity tend to have been raised within an intact family. These are not absolutes but they are significant correlations. These are correlations which are obvious and emphasize the importance of minimizing disturbances to intact families. Relationships can be difficult and challenges arise which force individuals to sacrifice their desires or wants for the benefit of the family. Once we have children our priorities must align with their best interest because those children deserve the very best start we can give them. Sometimes that means we must depart from bad habits and abandon destructive cultural beliefs we clung so tightly to. We only ever get one chance with our children. One chance to provide a loving, nurturing, supportive and stable environment for our children who will observe us overcome challenges and demonstrate honesty and kindness toward others which cultivates the moral and ethical standards within children that we would like them to have as adults.

"If we could change ourselves, the tendencies in the world would also change. As a man changes his own nature, so does the attitude of the world change towards him."

-Gandhi

LOVE

Love does not celebrate iniquity or devise evil things.

It doesn't walk about puffed up or envy your rings.

It doesn't behave rudely or seek it's own,

parade itself about or possess a provoked tone.

Love does, however, suffer long and is kind,

rejoices in truth and bears all without mind.

Believing and hoping, enduring life's merciless gales

and always remember, love never fails.

"In times of universal deceit, telling the truth is a revolutionary act."

-Unknown

www.ingramcontent.com/pod-product-compliance
Lightning Source LLC
Chambersburg PA
CBHW061205180526
45170CB00002B/962